The Five Traits of a Great Leader

Gerry M Hartigan

Published by the GHI Group

ISBN-13: 978-1463578183
ISBN-10: 1463578180
Revised version © 2016

Other Books by Gerry Hartigan

Yes You Can
The Five Traits of a Great Father
The Keys to an Abundant Life
The Keys to an Abundant Life Workbook
Millionaires Don't Have Stinkin' Thinkin'
God Can't Send Himself to Hell
An Irishman's Guide to Romance
The President is Dead (novel)
Common Sense Guide to Building Personal Wealth

Available at online booksellers and at:
http://gerryhartigan.com

The Five Traits of a Great Leader

Be the kind of person people follow

Gerry Hartigan

Acknowledgements

I want to thank all the people in my life who have been examples of leadership to me. From my father to people I have worked with, many have shown me the right way to lead and inspire others and I dedicate this book to them.

Table of Contents

"Remember the difference between a boss and a leader. A boss says go, a leader says let's go."

E.M. Kelly

Introduction

If you visit any bookstore or library, you will find hundreds of books on leadership and most of them are very good. Why another one? Over the last twenty years, I have traveled to over eighty countries and gained a vast amount of knowledge and experience that I share with my audiences. Having traveled to many countries and spoken to audiences in colleges, seminars, conferences and events, I have had the privilege of being around wonderful people who taught me life-changing things.

What I've learned from being a leader, and watching other people around leaders, is that *PEOPLE OBEY MANAGERS BUT THEY FOLLOW LEADERS.*

The purpose of this book is to help all of us who are in, or desire to be in, managerial positions, switch to being great leaders. Some managers suck at their job. We just have to face facts and admit it is true. Sometimes senior management doesn't want to hire men or women who are a threat to them and their position so they hire those who are less qualified and less experienced. This is a bad idea. Companies become great companies because of highly skilled leadership. Being a great leader means you know how to lead others and make decisions quickly and wisely. Don't allow your vision and decision-making become clouded due to insecurity. You will face the consequences because you are not hiring the best people. Without those qualified workers, the company has a more difficult time rising to the top.

I believe the following five traits are what makes a great leader. Am I saying there are only five traits? Of course not, but these five are crucial to having great success in management.

I decided to put all the principles in a short book. I do explain each principle in detail and even though it is a short book, it is full of great insights and nuggets to help you become a great leader.

I mention points that maybe others don't mention when talking about leadership. To me, these five areas are critical to your success as a leader. I hope you will learn something from this book, but more importantly, that you will apply a lot of what you learn here to help you become a better leader, manager, and business owner.

Read each chapter and see how it applies to your life and business. Avoid having a knee-jerk reaction because for many of us, our first reaction might be the wrong way. For instance, you may think you are an encouraging leader but take time to analyze how you react to situations. How do you deal with employees? Do you look for ways to bring out the best in them and help them reach their full potential? Do you encourage them in public but correct them in private? Or are you the kind of boss who shouts at your workers thinking that will make them work better? We all know the results that kind of leadership gets, so please try and avoid being a shouter; it won't get you anywhere but down the road to a lot of employee turnover.

What stage are you at in your managerial career? Have you started yet or is it a goal of yours? I hope that as you read these pages you will find nuggets of information that will help you reach your goal. As someone who has managed small teams and large teams, I believe I have learned through trial and error, what some of the best components of leadership are. The idea is to help you avoid this long learning process. You achieve that by applying the following principles into your management style and eventually have the employees see you as a leader and a manager.

If you are stuck in a work situation where you have a bad manager maybe you can mail him or her a copy of this book secretly and hope that he or she reads it. You never know, it could change things in your workplace. Bad managers often don't believe they are weak at their job. Quite the opposite. Some of them think they are great managers. It is this kind of delusional thinking that keeps people from becoming great managers and leaders.

Do I believe all managers are leaders? No! Are all leaders' managers? No! You can be a leader without having any responsibility to manage people or projects. You can be a leader with your brothers and sisters, or co-workers, or friends. A leader is someone who inspires others to take action and follow. A manager is someone who is responsible for getting projects done using people, machines and time.

I realize a large percentage of managers and leaders are women but to avoid using he/she every time I will just use he to make the book easier to read. In the United States today women are taking their rightful place running companies and starting large and very profitable companies themselves. Many of these women are exceptional examples of great leaders and we should all emulate them.

As we take a look at the role of a manager and then a leader, keep in mind that you may not see your weaknesses at first. It might take other people, like me, pointing out some things that you may not like to hear. That is good for all of us to hear now and again because we can have blind spots and not be aware that we are failing as a leader even though we may be a good manager and bringing in great results for our company.

The five traits I discuss are all learnable and can be implemented in your life and career fairly quickly so stay with me.

There is no exercise
better for the heart than
reaching down and
lifting people up."

John Holmes

The Encouraging Leader

A leader must be an encourager. Why is it so rare in some of those who hold senior management positions in companies? A grumpy, short-tempered manager seems to be far more common than an encouraging manger. What do I mean by an encouraging leader? I mean that he must go out of his way to encourage and build up those people he leads.

What do I mean by encouragement? To me, it means lifting up or patting someone on the shoulder to equip them to keep going and do a great job. Every person on the planet has several needs but let me highlight three of them.

1. **The need to be needed.**
2. **The need to be useful.**
3. **The need to be appreciated**.

The men and women you lead or manage have all three of these qualities. You and I have these same needs. You don't' believe me? Ask yourself, what are you looking for in life? What kind of appreciation do you want to receive from others? I bet when you think about it, you want the same things as everyone else. You want to be needed by your friends, family, and workers. Don't you want to feel useful? Do you want to leave a lasting legacy with your family and your community? That is why it is hard for entrepreneurs to retire. They feel like they are not contributing so they get frustrated and end up going back to work.

When you think about the people you lead, focus on those three areas and ask yourself how you can help them fulfill those needs and provide them a happy and productive environment. How can you help employees to feel needed? What words can you say to them when they do a good job or show up on time every day or go out of their way to go the extra mile at work? You won't notice these actions if you don't pay attention or have your other managers pay attention. Once these actions have been noted, take the time to bring those employees aside and thank them for their hard work and extra effort. When possible, make the praise public and speak highly of such employees. Morale will be boosted. You cannot possibly fathom how well employees receive this kind of encouragement. Just a simple sentence of thanks and appreciation from you will let the workers know that they are being noticed and this can only encourage them to do a good job and even try harder.

Emphasize to the employees how much their contribution matters to the business. Make a habit of reinforcing good behavior and showing and telling your workers they make a difference. Not from time to time, but on a regular basis. Each day, find ways to encourage your workers. Make a fuss of their efforts and praise them in public. Correct in private but always praise in public. Recognition and praise will do more for a person's productivity than any salary increase will.

No employee wants to be singled out for failure but every employee, and manager, wants to be singled out for praise. Praise has the effect of giving the other workers a lift too. They see how hard work gets rewarded and it encourages them to work hard. Public ridicule or correction has the opposite effect. It makes workers feel discouraged and they clam up. They will become disgruntled and lose a lot of their momentum to work harder. Why should they bother if all they get is public criticism when the make a mistake?

I'm in a McDonald's restaurant at 6:00 a.m. to order some breakfast, as I was heading out of town, I was about third in line to order my food when the manager came out from behind the cooking area and berated the cashier for being late. All of this was expresed in a loud voice with no regard to the fact that there were customers a few feet away listening to the tirade. Obviously, this manager, who might have also been the owner, was a complete and total idiot for acting as he did.

The cashier, a young teenage girl, took off her McDonalds cap, threw it on the ground, and in flowery language told the manager where to go. She stormed out of the restaurant. As she left she said in a harsh tone that she quit. Do you blame her?

I existed the restaurant, as did the other customers. The manager/owner was left with a dilemma as he was now short-staffed. I am sure that the rest of the employees were plotting their next job as it was obvious this man would have a tough time keeping employees. Do you see any of this scenario in your leadership style? Are you this kind of manager? If so we have some work to do to get you up to scratch. Don't despair, all things are possible. It is never too late to make changes for the better.

Now back to the example of the girl in McDonalds.

The girl may have deserved the reprimand but she didn't deserve public humiliation and this unskilled manager will have an unfruitful career ahead of him if he didn't learn how to correct in private and praise in public. Do you know of any managers or leaders who act like this? Unfortunately, most of us do, and some of you probably work for someone like this. Why are some in management such lousy examples of leadership? It may be because they get results that satisfy the owners. It could be because they are related to the owners or may even be the owners. I do not deny the fact that bad managers can get results. What I believe though is that good leaders get far better results than mediocre or crummy leaders. The good is the enemy of the best and your goal is to be the best leader you can be. That is not a difficult goal to reach once you learn the qualities that make a good leader, and more importantly, put them into action in your life and career.

Encouragement will get more results than the opposite. Just ask anyone you work with what they think of bosses who don't encourage them. I'm sure you will hear choice words come out of their months.

Now, how do you become an encourager?

Let me suggest ways that will ensure you become a more effective encouraging leader in the workplace.

1. ***Learn to be a good listener***. Not just someone who hears but someone who listens to what others are saying. Make eye contact with the person talking; that communicates respect and attention. It shows the speaker that you are focused on what they are saying. You help to make them feel appreciated. Listening to them will have the effect of making them more open and honest. You will learn far more if you learn to be a good listener.

   I worked for a boss that had the annoying habit of looking over your shoulder while you talked as if he was looking at something else. I never had the feeling that he was paying attention to anything I was saying. Obviously, this was very discouraging to me as I am sure it was to others too. This type of behavior can be a sign of insecurity in the leader or just plain rudeness. You need to avoid this habit and practice focusing your attention on what others are saying.

2. ***Learn patience***. Not everyone has the same personality as you. Not everyone acts the same way you do or thinks the same way you do. A great leader learns patience with others, as you want them to have patience with you. Allow others time to grow and time to make mistakes. We should learn from mistakes. Being a great a leader does not mean you don't make mistakes, it means you learn from them.

3. ***Honesty.*** In our world today, where the public is mistrusting of Wall Street as well as politicians, it is hard to gain people's trust because they are doubtful about your honesty. It's something you must nurture and exercise on a consistent basis.

The best way to do this is to be honest with your employees. You won't be able to share every detail of what is going on with your company but you should share as much as you possibly can to help them feel like they are part of a team and they matter to the company.

4. *Empathy*. You must learn to see things from someone else's perspective so you can see the whole picture. Try and put yourself in their shoes.

   It is easy for us to judge people when they do something wrong. The reason we fall into that trap is because we don't know what they are going through at the moment. We don't know what their situation is and what led up to them making the mistakes or doing something wrong.

   Empathy is trying to see an action from the other person's perspective. Are they sick, or going through a bad relationship or do they have financial problems? Many issues can lead to our actions and if we pause to think about these characteristics in other people, we may not be so quick to judge them.

5. *Decisive.* You must learn to make decisions and to make them well. Be decisive in your decision-making process. Don't be wishy-washy. Don't meander or vacillate. Instead, be

confident in your decision-making ability and go ahead and make the decision. Get as much advice and input as you think you need beforehand but after that, it is up to you to make the final choice as to the direction you are to head.

Once you master these characteristics of a good encourager you will be far more effective as a leader. Your employees will respond better to your decisions; they will be more confident in your leadership, and the organization will most likely be more productive and profitable. Efficiency will increase and morale will increase as workers know you will listen to them and they can rely on you to encourage them when they have done a good job.

It isn't rocket science, yet it amazes me how managers and leaders ignore these points and still try and get the best out of employees. It is not going to work unless you use fear and in the Western World that probably is not going to work very well.

Take time to take a hard look at your managerial style. Do you want to be the kind of person who inspires confidence and admiration from your employees? I know I do. It's rewarding to hear your employees thank you for the way you behave and the way you lead. Several times in my managerial career I have had the privilege of hearing positive feedback about my managerial role. It is fulfilling to me to know that others are inspired by me to do better work. What else can you ask for if you are a boss?

Don't allow pride to get in the way of applying these principles to your leadership style. Good men and women have burned out because of pride. Your employees will know if you are the cocky, stubborn type, who does not like to be wrong and will never admit it. Bad idea. If you make a mistake publicly, then accept the responsibility publicly and apologize. Then everyone that even you make mistakes although you thought you were immune. Put some humor into it. Make fun of yourself. You will come across as being more human and approachable. Your employees will enjoy coming to work more if you behave this way. They are also less likely to look for another job if they are happy where they are. You, as the manager/leader, play a huge part in their job satisfaction so look for ways to make their daily duties more enjoyable. It is not that hard to do. It takes a little bit of effort but like most things we work on, it brings great results. Try it, if its not part of your character right now.

"Life is ten percent what happens to you, and ninety percent how you respond to it.

Lou Holtz

The Aware Leader

What is an aware leader? Someone who notices what is going on in the lives of his employees. Someone who takes note of the actions of his employees and someone who keeps up to date with his industry, his competition, and his customers. To be an aware leader means you care about what is going on around you and notice how the work is affecting everyone under your leadership.

It helps if you are also emphatic like I mentioned in the previous chapter because then you will care about what is going on with your employees. How many bosses get a degree at college and then stop learning. They feel they have enough knowledge to last them the rest of their lives so there is no more need for further training or education. All the information they need can be acquired through reading the Wall Street Journal or the New York Times.

Being aware also means that you know your business well and what trends are taking place in your industry. There is no point in being a leader if you do not grow in your knowledge and understanding. To be effective you must be a learner and a good student of your business. To be aware of what is happening outside of the confines of your own business. Networking with other leaders in your field. Attending seminars, watching business channels, and reading key newspapers and magazine all help to make you an informed and aware leader in your field.

Too often managers behave and manage their business as if they have learned enough about their industry. They believe they can get by on their existing knowledge and still be an informed leader.

"In times of drastic change, it is the learners who inherit the future while the learned will find themselves beautifully equipped to deal with a world that no longer exists."
Eric Hoffer

What a powerful quote from Hoffer. One that every leader needs to heed. If you rest on your laurels and your existing knowledge the world will pass you by and you will find that your knowledge has become obsolete. Don't let that happen to you. The way to avoid that is to learn constantly. Seek for new knowledge and new understanding in all aspects of your life and work. I read at least one book a week and listen to two audio programs a month in my car. That means that every day I am learning something new about my business, about life, and about myself. I want to be aware of who I am and what is happening in the world around me so I can be a better person and a better leader.

A few years ago a small business owner asked me to take a look at his business and recommend improvements on how the business was run and see if I could come up with an effective marketing plan to help them grow to the next level of success. I spent a day at the business and observe how it was functioning. I interviewed a lot of the employees to ask about their job functions and if they had any ideas as to how to improve performance. As I expected, many of them did have great suggestions. The people doing the work are the best place to start if you want to come up with innovative ideas to improve quality and productivity. A week later I came back to the business with my report and recommendations. My meeting that day was with the owner and his father, who was the founder of the business. I soon discovered that even though dad was 'retired' he still had a major say in the running of the operation. It was evident by the way he treated his son and assumed control of the proceedings very quickly.

After I had given my report and made my recommendations the son attempted to make a comment but his father butted in and said, *"We're not interested in making any of these changes. Our company has been making money for fifty years quite fine without outside help and we will do the same for another fifty years. The meeting is over."*

He got up and left the room leaving his son speechless and embarrassed. To say I was shocked is an understatement. The son did his best to smooth over the incident but he sheepishly thanked me for my time and effort and assured me my check for payment would be in the mail. He also sheepishly said they would not be able to implement my suggested changes at this time. He then apologized for his father's behavior and said he had thought his dad would be more receptive to innovation and chances to grow the business but he was wrong.

I left that meeting shaking my head but at the same time I understood where the father was coming from and why it was hard for him to accept my suggestions. Change is never easy for any of us. Change that is radical is even more difficult.

If you want to be the best leader possible accept the fact that you will be a life-long learner. You can't communicate new truths to others if you do not learn them first yourself. A leader can only lead people to where he or she is. That is what gives us the incentive as leaders to learn and grow. You can't teach someone a truth that you don't know or a skill you have not acquired so be a constant learner.

Being an aware leader also means knowing your weaknesses and the weaknesses of your business. Every business should do a *SWOT* analysis every year or two. Many companies make SWOT a crucial part of their evaluation process and it applies to companies and individuals. So if you are a manager or owner you should implement a SWOT on a regular basis to keep your company informed and competitive. What is SWOT?

Strengths
Weaknesses
Opportunities
Threats

What are your businesses strengths? Do you even know what they are? Have you ever taken the time even to think about them? Some of your strengths might be price, exclusivity, or service. It might be hard for you to articulate them but you need to be able to define what they are for the sake of the growth of your business.

What do I mean by weaknesses? If you are a small retain business located near a Wal-Mart, one of your weaknesses may be the price. You may not be able to compete with the big boys on the issue of price so don't try.

What are your weaknesses? Think about it for a few minutes and write down what comes into your head. Some of your company's weaknesses might be its location, or price, or your inventory. There can be any number of issues that contribute to your weaknesses. What can you do to strengthen your weaknesses or even get rid of them altogether? Weakness may be the quality of your staff due to the low salaries you offer. It might be time to think about upping your game and hiring more qualified but more expensive workers to work for you. They should bring experience, knowledge, and creativity along with their higher wages and it should increase your service to customers, the quality of your products and your profits.

Sometimes business owners are reluctant to spend more money as times are tight. But if one of your weaknesses as a business is the quality of those who work for you, through lack of experience and skills, then that weakness needs to be addressed. You may need to hire better-qualified employees. It will cost you more money in salaries and benefits but it should also bring greater productivity and sales. Of course you ensure that the people you hire are worth the money. Give every new employee a ninety-day probation period that allows you to part ways with them if they don't meet your requirements. A period of ninety-days is long enough for a highly qualified person to show whether they are worth the money or not.

As the leader, you oversee this type of work through delegated personnel. Check on new employees often with their supervisors if they do not report to you directly. Workers can languish in jobs without performing and get away with it for quite some time. Unproductive employees can end up costing the company a lot of money and waste a lot of precious time. You will be ticked if company money is wasted in this way. Don't allow unproductive employees to be one of your company's weaknesses.

You need to guard against discrimination when it comes to hiring employees. As a man do you have a preference for male management staff, even if they are not the most qualified? This can rob your company of the knowledge, experience and skills of a highly competent female manager so check yourself to ensure you are not bringing your personal prejudices into the business. Maybe you only want to hire people who are less skilled or educated than you are to ensure they never look better than you at meetings when they share with other managers and staff. A dangerous trait among owners and managers that is far too common.

A few years ago I was being considered as a speaker at a symposium at a university. A friend of mine had recommended me to the staff at the university that were planning the event. It seemed that I had far more qualification than they were looking for and therefore would be a good candidate as a speaker. I was not offered the speaking slot and in speaking with my friend a few months later I discovered that the person hired to speak was nowhere near as qualified as I was for that topic but he knew the organizer. In business this kind of managing that can affect your bottom line. Your sales, profits, employee morale, and overall health of the business is ALWAYS affected by the kind of leadership running the company. So be extra careful to hire the best people for the position even if they are more qualified than you are. When they succeed and the company becomes more profitable, you will look good for your great wisdom in hiring that person.

As the aware leader you now are you will try and avoid such mistakes and look for the best opportunities for your company to grow and become more profitable.

Do you have room for growth as a business? Can you obtain more products to sell? Can you partner with another business to increase your market share? Think about the opportunities you can create for your business. You may not like the idea of partnering with others but it could be the key to real growth. You get access to their markets as they get access to yours but you should be able to complement one another and not be a threat to them or to you. Successful entrepreneurs realize that to grow, you have to reach out to others and form partnerships. That can be a good thing so don't be afraid of it.

What are the threats to your business? Is a Wal-Mart opening nearby? Are better known businesses moving to the area? Customers tastes change which may mean your products are no longer in fashion. You have to learn to adapt to the mood of the market. Threats can come in all shapes and sizes. Think about Blockbuster. Who would have thought they would go out of business and lose their market share? In their heyday, the only way to go was up because they had no competition to speak of when they were riding high on top of the world. Along came Netflix and then Redbox and all of a sudden you are not the main kid on the block anymore.

Competition can jump into the game at a moment's notice so be thinking of what is coming down the road that will affect your business.

By checking your business every year using a *SWOT* analysis you will be up to date on how your business is doing in relation to others in your industry. It is also a good idea as a leader to do a *SWOT* exam on yourself. Might be hard for you but it needs to be done so that you can grow as a person and a leader.

What are your personal strengths, weaknesses, opportunities, and threats? Don't allow pride to get in the way of this. Pride is a killer when it comes to expanding your business and motivating your employees. By knowing your limitations you will know where you need to hire. Bill Gates hired people who knew more than he did about computers and software, programs. What is the point of hiring men and women who know what you already know? You want people who can expand your business through their talent and skills. They are not a threat to you because they know more you do. They are a great asset and every successful business owner knows the truth of this principle.

Be a student of life and your market. Read journals on a regular basis. Attend conferences and seminars where you can gain wisdom from others who will help you expand your vision. Listen to your employees. They will help your business greatly if you take the time to listen to them. Think of the fact that your employees have been with you for several years; some since you started your business. Imagine the depth of experience they have accumulated and are able to share with you and your management team.

Being an aware leader also means knowing when it is time to let some employees go. It is never easy to fire anyone but an aware leader knows what is best for the company and which employees are helping and which ones are hindering. Often management can allow weak employees to stay on to avoid conflict. No one wants to put a person in the unemployment line so weak or unqualified employees can last a lot longer than they should. This may sound cruel but remember you are not running a charity; you are running a business and a business has to make money to make it worthwhile. The longer weak employees stay on the payroll the more profit your business is losing. As an aware leader, it is your responsibility to make the tough decisions.

I worked under a manager one time whose way of dealing with problems was to form a committee to look into the problem. The committee was to take a week to look into the situation and report back to management. Then, instead of making a decision, my boss would throw something else at the committee to look into concerning the problem. This just prolonged the decision but got him off the hook for a while. A trait like this is a sign of weak leadership and is not good for the company. Passing the buck is a cheap way of avoiding conflict and decision-making. Unless you own the company you won't last too long in your position if you keep behaving like this. Learn to make the tough decisions.

Next we will look at the decision maker. Making decisive decisions a crucial role of a good leader.

"When I take action, I'm not going to fire a $2 million dollar missile at a $10 empty tent and hit a camel in the butt. It's going to be decisive."

George W. Bush

The Decisive Leader

Can you make decisions quickly and with confidence? Not foolish decision based on a whim but after looking at all the facts and information can you take the responsibility and make the decision that is needed for the staff to move forward with accomplishing their roles.

You must be a decisive leader in order to inspire confidence in those you lead. There is nothing worse in the workplace than working under an indecisive leader. Employees are never quite sure what they are supposed to be doing, as the signals they get from management are confusing and contradictory. Productivity will suffer drastically if you as a leader cannot make decisions and make them quickly. You have to be able to analyze a situation and make a decision based on the facts presented to you.

A decisive leader is not necessarily an impulsive leader. An impulsive leader doesn't listen to others; doesn't gather all the facts first. A decisive leader will listen to input from others and gather all the facts but then make a decision quickly so the business can move forward. There is a big difference between the two styles of leadership. From the previous characteristic of being an aware leader the more aware you are the more decisive you will become. One leads on to the other. As an effective leader you must also develop the skill of being able to evaluate situations as they are presented to you; gather the facts, listen to others; and then make a decision. Your business cannot go forward until you make the decisions that your employees can implement. That is your responsibility as the decision maker.

How do you develop your skill as a decision maker? Several ways can help.

1. **Trust your instincts**. It is your business and no one cares about it as much as you do. You are the only one who truly lives or dies by your business. If you are managing for someone else than that means you have a responsibility to the owners to be decisive. They didn't hire you to be wishy-washy. They hired you to make them money and lots of it. The longer you take the make wise decision, the less money you are making for them and boy will they be pissed at you for that.

   Trust your own abilities. Lean on your experience but also the wisdom and experience of others and see how they made a similar decision in the past.

2. **Learn from others**. Watch and learn from other leaders as to how they lead companies and what kind of decision-

making skills they have and how did they acquire them. You must pay attention to your industry and see how other managers and business owners are making decisions. Read lots of biographies of men and women you admire who have gone before you. They have much to teach all of us and we need to learn from their successes and their failures.

3. **Take Action**. Realize that nothing gets done until you take action. Your business will remain stagnant if you do not take the lead. Taking action will challenge you to become a skilled decision maker. One you have taken action and made a decision, believe in it. Follow through to ensure it is implemented the way you feel is right and don't let go of it unless it is not working. Then you can move on to make a different decision which you hope will work.

4. **Seek advice**. Ask for advice and input. Learn to weigh up various opinions. By understanding what other people think you will learn to decipher the multitude of ideas and thoughts that are presented to you.

Don't be a Lone Ranger. Understand that working with a team will produce far greater results than you working on your own so seek own the counsel, wisdom and advice of others. Listen to the experience of those around you and those you lead.

5. **Practice.** Practice making decisions. Start small but practice it. It might sound silly to you but for many managers making good decisions is not easy. They are great at making rash decisions or flippant ones, but making great decisions is hard for them. That's why practicing good decisions is necessary.

   Practice will involve the process of good decision-making. That includes, patience, listening to others, getting all the facts and advice and then making a solid decision. If this is a problem for you then you definitely have to practice making good ones.

6. **Make the tough decisions first**. If you have to fire someone for the good of the company then do it quickly. Do it with concern for your employees' situations of course but nevertheless, the decisions have to be made and you are the one to make them.

   You may think you should make the easy decisions first but I disagree. I believe if you fight the giants first you mind will be a lot clearer and more focused. This will allow you to press forward with more confidence as you make more decisions.

That assurance of your ability to make decisions will only increase as you use wisdom and the wisdom you learn from others, to continue on in your leadership and management career.

7. **Don't live in the past**. Once you have made the decision, move on. Some of your decisions will be good and some will be not so good. Once they are made you must move on. Some you will be able to correct and implement new directions but others have to be left allowed. Know the difference.

8. **Accept your decision**. Use what you have learned to ensure your future decisions will be more accurate if you made a bad choice. Make sure you soak in all the lessons learned so you don't repeat the mistakes.

Don't allow pride to rob you of learning from your mistakes. We all know many managers who have a lot of pride and arrogance. How they have jobs is beyond me but we have to put up with them on a daily basis so don't be one of those duds. Be an example of a solid leader. A leader who is humble, learns from his mistakes and acknowledges them in front of others.

A decisive leader is not arrogant in his decision making. Rather, he is considerate of others and takes into account the feelings of others. At the same time realizing that the good of the company is your responsibility. Your decisions have to be weighed with that ultimate thought in mind.

Imagine how hard it is to be the President of the United States and the pressure that is on that person to make wise decisions. Whatever the President decides can have far reaching impact, not only in the United States, but around the world. That is a little bit different than the decisions that most of us have to make on a daily basis.

Fortunately, most of us don't have that kind of pressure on us when we make decisions but we need to treat decision-making as an important part of our roles as leaders. Being decisive is not a license to be insensitive. You have a responsibility to the people you lead. You take their welfare into consideration when you make a decision for your business and see how it will affect them.

Can lay-offs be avoided if you take a different path? Can you reorganize your staff to put them in different positions that will allow them to be more productive? Don't assume that firing someone to save money is the best thing to do. What about staff morale after a bunch of lay-offs? You can bet your life on the fact that a lot of your employees will be dusting off their resumes and applying for other jobs if a bunch of their friends just got laid off.

As an aware leader there is a lot on your plate. People's livelihoods and their emotional states, are affected by the choices you make as their manager. You have tremendous power for good and for bad. So be aware of the people who work for you. Be aware of the industry you are in. Continue to better yourself as a person and as a business leader. Keep in touch with others in your field and learn from them. Most people are happy to share lessons they have learned if they feel the person asking has a genuine interest.

The more aware you are, the more effective you will be. Your people will appreciate that as one of your skills if you apply yourself in this area. Don't slack off. Always be a learner and always possess an inquisitive mind. Those are the kind of people who progress in life a lit bit faster than the rest of us. That zest to learn will help you change lives and change your world.

"Generosity is giving more than you can, and pride is taking less than you need."

Khalil Gibran

The Generous Leader

A great leader is a generous leader. Generous with their time, their praise and their finances. A generous leader inspires loyalty and confidence in his workers because they know they will be fairly compensated for their hard work.

Think about your work situation. If you work for a company that is tight with its money and rarely gives raises, how does that affect your moral and your work ethic? It's very discouraging and you have a difficult time putting your heart and soul into your work because you feel it won't be noticed or rewarded. Bosses like this also have a lot of employee turnover for obvious reasons. Learn to be a generous leader. Research has shown that companies that do reward their employees often and even allow them to share in the profits, will be far more productive than companies that don't operate this way. Yet the vast majority of businesses still strive to keep the last time for their bosses and shareholders, instead of sharing the success with the people who actually make the company work, the employees.

It is not that difficult to have a paradigm shift as to how to reward and treat your workers.

It just takes a conscious choice to treat them as a major part of the organization, without whom, a lot of the real work never gets done. When you think of the business owners, managers and employees as one unit, it becomes easy to see the need to include everyone in the growth and success of the company. Employee loyalty and work ethic increases dramatically when employees feel a stake in the company

As a generous leader you will begin to observe how your business grows and the quality of the work improves.

Here are ideas to help you become that kind of special leader the world needs more of today.

1. Give generous praise to those deserving of it. Single them out for recognition and thanks for their contribution to your business.
2. Give bonuses and raises regularly. I know it cuts into your profits but in reality, it increases your profits because the happier your employees are the harder they work and that makes them more productive which should make your business more profitable.
3. Sponsor charitable events in your community like a Little League team or

fundraiser. Make your business known as a company that cares about their social responsibility. Engage your workers to take part in these events on a voluntary basis.

4. Set up scholarships for economically disadvantaged kids in your community. For $500 or even $5,000 each.

5. Give of your time to help worthwhile causes. Your heart will feel good, your spirit will be encouraged, and your business will receive a lot of very positive publicity. But don't do it for that reason. Do it because you care about other people, otherwise, they will see right through your phoniness and that will put your business down the tubes.

6. Offer benefits to employees that most other companies don't, like childcare, or a nurse on duty or a counselor for troubled employees. Initiate a three-month paid leave program for new mothers.

7. Organize regular picnics and other such events for employees and their families to build up appreciation and a sense of belonging somewhere.

Most employees state that job satisfaction is more important than more money. If one of your employees is offered a job elsewhere with a bigger salary, there is a good chance they will turn it down if they have high job satisfaction at your business. Money is not the main factor in job-hopping.

None of the items mentioned above are that difficult for your business to accomplish but they will have far-reaching effects in getting your business known and building up loyalty in your staff. Without your staff, you have no business. Treat them with respect and show your generosity for all that they do to make you successful.

"Gratitude can turn common days into thanksgivings, turn routine jobs into joy, and change ordinary opportunities into blessings."

William Arthur Ward

The Thankful Leader

An unusual trait to see in a book about leadership? I don't think it should be. A great leader is a thankful leader. Thankful for all the blessings in his life and business. It is a proven fact that thankful people lead happier and more abundant lives. Therefore, it stands to reason that thankful leaders should lead more productive lives and have more productive businesses. Think I am crazy?

Take a look at the business world today. Analyze the lives of the most successful men and women. Which ones are leading the most productive lives? I didn't say which ones are the richest. Money has nothing to do with it. I asked which of them are leading productive and fulfilling lives. You will usually find that it is those who are grateful for everything and everyone they have in their lives. They are thankful for their employees, their families, their customers, and their wealth. They know that it takes an army of people to make their world go around and they never lose sight of that. Being grateful gives them a heads-up on their competition.

A leader with a thankful attitude will have an encouraging effect on his employees. The employees will respond positively to the boss's behavior. They will enjoy their work more which means they will be more productive. A lot of these ideas sound like common sense but as we all know common sense is not all that common. It is sad to say that too often leaders and business owners neglect their employees and only care about the almighty dollar. You have to be concerned about profits and income but not at the expense of people. Try and learn to have a balance.

Being thankful helps you to have a more positive outlook on life and business. It helps you to look at situations with a better perspective and this can only help you be a more effective leader. If you go to work every day with a grumpy attitude then that will show up in your decision-making and the way you treat workers. Others will feed off your negativity and that is not good. Not good for you, not good for them and not good for your business. Check your attitude at the door to ensure that it is a positive one before you start your day. It is your money that is at stake so learn to be thankful for all that you have in life and in business and it will reap great rewards.

If your business is making a profit every year isn't that something to be ecstatic about and be truly thankful? With many businesses and individuals struggling to survive and make ends meet, you should certainly see the point of being thankful. Try to focus on what you have instead of what you don't have. Maybe you don't have 50% growth but if you have 5% growth your company is still heading in the right direction.

Maybe you don't drive a Mercedes but your car gets you from point A to point B. What more do you want from the piece of metal? The car won't make you important or successful. It may appear to others you are, but the only opinion about you that matters is yours. Live your life to please you, and only you. Count your blessings as an individual. Count your blessings as a business owner or manager. Be thankful for the employees who show up to work every day and work hard for eight hours or more to make your company successful and profitable.

"I wish I had spent more time at the office."

These words have never been written on anyone's headstone after they have died. Yet, many wealthy people who can afford lots of breaks, do everything they can to work 70 to 80 hours a week and sacrifice their health, family and loved ones, to make their business more successful.

A few years ago I read an interview in a business magazine. The man being interviewed was a very well-known successful businessman. The magazine stated that his net worth was over $400,000,000. The man was asked how often he took vacations. He had young children. The man laughed it off and said he hated vacations. He was in his office six days a week and sometimes seven. His family took vacations without him. To me, this is a very sad man. Yes, he is a very wealthy man in terms of money, but a very sad man in terms of real wealth. I agree with hard work to make your business succeed but when you have already accumulated $400,000,000 I think you can say to yourself that you are successful and you can take vacation time.

A good balance is to try and take family vacation weekends several times a year and major vacations at least twice a year. You will be a lot healthier for it, your family will be stronger, your wife and children will be happier, and you will be much more fulfilled as a person and a leader.

In the work place thankfulness will show up when an employee brings you a glass of water or coffee, or works late without extra pay to finish a project, or goes out of their way to make you and the company look good. It is crucial in such instances that you utter words of thanks and if possible, do something to thank the person. Make it a regular habit to thank employees for their hard work and commitment. Make a fuss of them and praise them in meetings, seminars, retreats, and in print if you give interviews. Always be thankful in your mind and heart and it will easily come out in life and work. It is not that hard and I am sure you have a gazillion things to be thankful for. Every morning as you get to your office take a few seconds to be thankful in your mind for the company, the staff, the leadership and the employees and all that they do to make your life comfortable. As a leader, you get a chance to lead those people but they bless your life in innumerable ways.

Be thankful in your mind for your customers and clients. Without them you have no job. Be thankful for your vendors and suppliers and every other person who contributes to making your job easier and successful. You will be amazed at how many people contribute to your success every day. Never take them for granted.

If your actions inspire others to dream more, learn more, do more and become more, you are a leader.

John Quincy Adams

SUMMARY

Just to recap what we have learned in this book.

1. Be an encourager not just at work but also in life in general.
2. Be aware of people around you and their needs and also what is going on in your industry.
3. Learn to be decisive. It does not mean you have to make decisions quickly but it does mean that you make them and learn to live with them.
4. Be generous with your time and praise. Give of yourself to others and let them know you care about them.
5. Be thankful for all the good things in your life and thankful for the men and women who work with you.

Good leaders lead by example. Take these five traits and incorporate them into your life and leadership style and you will be successful. Your relationship with your staff and co-workers will improve which can only mean that your health will improve due to less stress in your life. The productivity of your business or the company you work fun will increase as employees will be more fulfilled and desirous of doing a great job. The ball is in your court and you are the one who has to decide if these traits are worth implementing into your management style. I hope you agree they are worth it.

No man will make a great leader who wants to do it all himself or get all the credit for doing it.

Andrew Carnegie

About the Author

Gerry Hartigan was born and raised in Ireland and has traveled to over eighty countries. He holds a Master's Degree in Management and spoken throughout the world in seminars, conferences, events, businesses, and universities.

His management coaching programs have helped businesses grow and take their companies to the next level. Whether you need a keynote speaker or management training for your business, Gerry's relaxing style, Irish wit, and vast experience will ensure that your audience members leave with smiles on their faces and real challenges for their lives.

Gerry lives in Northern Virginia.
Contact him at info@gerryhartigan.com

http://gerryhartigan.com

www.ingramcontent.com/pod-product-compliance
Lightning Source LLC
Chambersburg PA
CBHW071252170526
45165CB00003B/1318